WE'LL NEVER FORGET YOU, ROBERTO CLEMENTE

BY TRUDIE ENGEL

SCHOLASTIC INC.
New York   Toronto   London   Auckland   Sydney
Mexico City   New Delhi   Hong Kong   Buenos Aires

P9-DBY-434

PHOTO CREDITS
Black-and-white interior photos:

UPI/Bettmann: pp. x, 24, 41, 51, 60, 66, 77, 107; The Bettmann Archive: p. 30; Office of Public Relations, Economic Development Administration: p. 4; Puerto Rico News Service: p. 10; Puerto Rico Office of Information, Photo by Rosskam: p. 19; Black Heritage Pittsburgh 1960/FPG: p. 45; AP/Wide World Photos: pp. 56, 72, 75, 94, 95; United Press International Photo: p. 82; El Dia, San Juan/National Baseball Hall Of Fame and Museum Inc.: p. 97.

ISBN-13: 978-0-590-68881-9
ISBN-10: 0-590-68881-2

Copyright © 1996 by Trudie Engel.
All rights reserved. Published by Scholastic Inc. SCHOLASTIC and associated
logos are trademarks and/or registered trademarks of Scholastic Inc.

48 47   18 19 20
Printed in the U.S.A.   40

First Scholastic printing, October 1996

Contents

Roberto Clemente was a great baseball star and a special hero to young fans.

Chapter 1
Born to Be a Baseball Player

Here comes the windup, the pitch.

It wasn't a ball that sailed toward the batter. It was an empty tomato soup can.

And Momen, the dark-skinned kid at the plate, wasn't swinging a bat. He held a broomstick in his hands.

Bam. The broomstick hit the can. It flew high into the sky.

Bam, bam, bam. Again and again, cans sailed into the air. Some hit the palm trees that stood at the edge of the field.

It was a simple game. One person is up at bat. The others all play in the

1

field. If you strike out, you have to pitch.

"My turn." A brown-skinned boy named Felipe now stood at the plate. He had a good swing, too. He sent soup cans flying into the trees.

But Felipe wasn't quite as good as Momen. He missed once in a while.

"Strike two," the pitcher yelled as Felipe's broomstick missed the can a second time. Then Felipe whiffed again. This was strike three.

Felipe trotted out into the field. He was the pitcher now.

Soon Momen was up again.

Bam, bam, bam. Felipe tried hard to strike him out, but Momen couldn't miss.

"I'll get you," called Felipe. "Watch this." He whizzed a can across the plate, and Momen's broomstick swung into the empty air. "Strike one!" yelled Felipe.

The next can came flying in. Momen missed again.

"Strike two!"

"I'm gonna get you now!" Felipe scooped up a can. "I'm gonna do it."

The tin can flew in high and fast.

But Momen's broomstick found it. *Wham!* The tin can disappeared into the palm trees.

Felipe shook his head. No one could strike out Momen.

When it was too dark to find the cans, the game was over. The boys started to make their way home. Momen did not have far to go. His house was across the street from the playground. The other boys began to walk back home slowly on the dusty, unpaved road that led up the hillside from the ball field.

"*Hasta mañana,*" Momen called out to his friends as he walked into his front yard. That means "See you tomorrow" in Spanish.

The island of Puerto Rico where Roberto grew up is a tropical paradise.

It was 1943 in Puerto Rico.

Puerto Rico is an island in the Caribbean Sea. It is part of the United States. Because Puerto Rico used to belong to Spain, the people speak Spanish, Spain's native language.

Spanish is spoken in many countries in the Western Hemisphere. People from those countries are called Latin Americans.

Many famous Latin American ballplayers have come from Puerto Rico. The weather there is so warm that baseball is played all year round.

The boy called Momen became the most famous of them all.

In 1943, Momen was nine years old, the youngest of seven children. One of his older sisters had given him the name Momen. It was just a made-up word that sounded cute. No one knew what it meant. Momen's real name was Roberto Clemente.

The Clemente family lived in a white, wooden house set back from the road in a grove of trees. The Puerto Rican summer night was quiet and dark. Very few houses had electricity.

Roberto's mother, Luisa, stood by the gate that evening, smelling the sweet air from the flowers that bloomed everywhere. She then saw Roberto crossing the road. He looked as happy as he always did after playing broom ball with his friends.

Luisa and Roberto went into the house. Roberto headed straight for his room.

Soon loud thumps and a crackling sound broke the stillness. Luisa smiled. She knew what these noises were. Roberto was on his bed, bouncing a rubber ball off his bedroom walls. His ear was close to a small radio. Roberto was listening to a ball game.

I know, Luisa thought to herself, that Roberto was born to be a baseball player.

Chapter 2
"Earn It"

Melchor Clemente, Roberto's father, could not read or write. He worked all his life on the large farms, called plantations, that grew sugarcane in Puerto Rico.

When Melchor Clemente was a boy, children as young as six had to work in the fields. There was no time to go to school. Families were large. If the children did not help earn money, there would not be enough food to eat.

Melchor Clemente wanted his children to have a better life than he had. He worked hard so that all the Clemente children could go to school.

The Clemente family did not have much money, but they were not as poor as many of the people who lived around them.

When Roberto was growing up, his father made four dollars a week as a foreman in charge of workers who cut the sugarcane.

Besides cutting sugarcane, he ran a small store that sold food to the workers. He also owned a truck that he rented out.

Luisa Clemente helped out as well. She washed clothes for the rich family who owned the sugar plantation.

When the Clemente children were not in school, they worked to help the family. Roberto and his brothers were hired by builders to load and unload sand and other building materials from their father's truck. In the summer, Melchor often took his children with him to work in the cane fields.

One hot summer day, Roberto and his father were working near the road that ran through the fields. The road went to San Juan, the biggest city in Puerto Rico.

Roberto and his father often worked together in sugar cane fields like this one.

Beep. Beep. A horn sounded. Melchor and Roberto looked up and watched a large, black car make its way toward them along the dusty road.

The car slowed down as it passed. Roberto could see an old, light-skinned man dressed in a white shirt and a tie sitting in the backseat. He was the owner of the plantation on his way to lunch at a fancy hotel in San Juan.

The plantation owner smiled and waved. But Melchor did not smile or wave back. He just nodded his head a little toward the old man as the car passed.

Roberto stared at the back of the car.

"Why didn't you wave, Papa?" he asked. "That was the big shot."

Melchor frowned. "Don't ever forget," he told Roberto, "he is no better than you."

Roberto never forgot.

On that day, the nine-year-old Roberto had something important on his mind.

"Papa," he said. "Can I have a bicycle?"

Melchor said nothing. The Clementes had just enough money to put food on the table and buy the clothes the children needed to go to school. There was nothing extra for a bicycle.

"Please, Papa." Roberto looked hopefully at his father. He wanted a bicycle almost as much as he wanted to be a baseball player.

"You must earn it, yourself," Melchor said.

Soon Roberto heard about a neighbor who needed someone to carry a heavy can of milk to his house from the store every day. The store was half a mile away. The man said he would pay three cents a day.

So every morning at six clock, the sleepy Roberto stumbled out of bed to get the milk. He lugged the can to the neighbor's house, took the pennies home, and tossed them into a glass jar his mother kept in the kitchen.

Luisa smiled as she heard the *plunk* of the coins landing in the jar day after day.

Slowly, the jar filled up. After two years, Roberto had enough money for a bicycle.

The bicycle was almost new. It was bright red. The paint was still shiny.

Roberto hopped on his bicycle. He wanted to show his father. He pedaled down the road that led to the sugarcane fields.

Soon the shiny red bike was covered with dust. But Roberto didn't care. When he saw Melchor bending over the cane, he shouted, "Papa, Papa! Look!"

Melchor looked up. Roberto waved to his father from the bicycle he had earned all by himself.

Melchor grinned and waved back. He had always told his children, "Be proud of who you are. Work hard. Pay your own way."

Melchor also believed in helping others who had even less than he had.

Life in Puerto Rico was hard, but the Clemente family would never let others go hungry.

Roberto Clemente learned all of his father's lessons well.

Chapter 3
"I Am Momen"

It was another soup can and broomstick game. A strange car pulled up by the playing field. The man behind the wheel was a baseball scout.

From under the palm trees, the scout watched a kid with powerful arms who never struck out. Then he waved the batter over to the car.

"Who are you?" he asked the dark-skinned boy.

"I am Momen," the boy said shyly.

The man leaned out the window and looked at the boy's large, strong hands.

"Come to town tomorrow," he said, "and try out for a team."

Roberto was fourteen years old. He had been on a youth league team since he was eight. But he had never played outside his neighborhood.

The tryout was for a softball team in San Juan. Roberto made the team. Soon he was the team's starting shortstop.

Roberto had his first uniform, a T-shirt with the name of the team written across the front.

Momen had become Roberto Clemente, ballplayer. He took his ball-playing very seriously.

He always had an old rubber ball with him. When he wasn't playing softball, he squeezed the ball to make his arms and hands stronger.

Roberto went to high school during the day. The softball games were played at night. Often the players went out together after a game.

Roberto sat with the team and listened to the talk. But while the others drank beer, he drank milk.

Roberto was also a star on his high school track team. His best event was the javelin throw. He threw the javelin so far, people said he was good enough to be in the Olympic Games.

But Roberto's first love was always baseball.

Many famous American baseball players came to Puerto Rico to play in the Puerto Rican Winter League. There was a big stadium in San Juan where the games were played.

Sometimes Roberto's father sent him to San Juan on the bus to buy

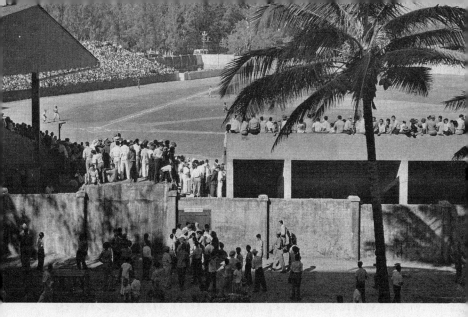

Roberto used to hang around the baseball stadium in San Juan hoping to see his favorite major league stars.

lottery tickets. Roberto would get off the bus at the stadium and stand outside.

He wanted to get a look at the major league stars. His big hero was Monte Irvin, a black player with a great arm.

One day a foul ball came flying over

the stadium wall. Roberto caught it and took it home.

He always thought that Monte Irvin may have hit that ball. It became one of Roberto's biggest treasures. No one else was allowed to play with it. He even slept with the ball at night to keep it away from his brothers.

Roberto's friends from high school remember that he was shy and very polite. When answering a question from his teacher, he looked down at the floor. This is how you show respect for older people in Spanish-speaking countries.

Roberto was a good student. His mother wanted him to go to college and become an engineer. But he never did. Baseball had become Roberto's whole life. When he got caught up in a game, he even forgot to go home for the good meals of pork, rice, and beans his mother cooked for him.

One night Luisa had had enough. Roberto came home too late for dinner again! To teach him a lesson, she threw his bat into the fire. But Roberto pulled the burning bat out of the fire and saved it.

He used his bat and glove to make all of Puerto Rico more proud of him than his mother could ever imagine.

Chapter 4
"One More"

In the spring of 1952, when Roberto was eighteen years old, a tryout was held in San Juan's baseball stadium.

Many scouts were looking over a group of young players. Some of the scouts were from the Santurce Crabbers, a team in the Puerto Rican Winter League. Others were from the Brooklyn Dodgers, a major league team in New York.

The players were lined up in center field, throwing to home. The scouts watched as the balls floated into home plate.

Suddenly, a ball shot in as straight and fast as an arrow.

The Brooklyn coach stared at the young black player who had sent the ball whizzing over the plate.

It was Roberto.

"*Uno más*, one more," shouted the scout.

Roberto did it again, and again, and again.

All the other players were sent home.

For the rest of the day, the scouts watched only Roberto. They asked him to throw, run, and hit.

"He's the greatest natural athlete I ever saw," said the Brooklyn scout.

He did not have enough experience to play for the Dodgers. Instead, Roberto was offered a position playing for the Santurce Crabbers.

From the beginning of his baseball career, Roberto Clemente wore number 21.

Roberto signed a contract to play with them. The team gave him a $400 bonus and paid him $40 a week.

Because Roberto was underage, Melchor Clemente had to sign the contract. He couldn't write his name, so he signed with an X.

Roberto played for the Crabbers for two winters. Many major leaguers were on the team. Roberto learned a lot.

He changed his batting style. And out in right field, he started to make his famous "basket catches." Instead of reaching up to grab the ball while it was still over his head, Roberto would wait until the ball fell to the level of his belt buckle. Then he caught it.

Roberto said, that the basket catch

made it easier to get off a fast, hard throw.

By 1954, many scouts from the major leagues were looking at Roberto. The Dodgers had not forgotten him. They offered him a $10,000 bonus to join their team.

No ballplayer from Latin America had ever been paid such a big bonus. The two best known Spanish-speaking players had gotten only $200 and $500.

An excited, happy Roberto agreed to join the Dodgers.

Then came some upsetting news. The Milwaukee Braves, another major league team, wanted Roberto to play for them. They said they would give him a $30,000 bonus.

What should he do? Roberto talked it over with his family. For the Clementes, honor was more important than money.

"If you gave the word, you keep the word," his mother said.

Roberto kept his word. He joined the Brooklyn Dodgers.

The Dodgers decided to send Roberto to Montreal, Canada, to play with the Montreal Royals. Montreal was the Dodgers most important minor league team.

Roberto was one step away from playing major league baseball.

His father saw him off at the San Juan airport. "Buy yourself a good car and don't depend on anyone," Melchor Clemente told his son.

It was Roberto's first airplane ride. He sat by the window and watched the green island of Puerto Rico get smaller and smaller. Soon it disappeared into the wide, blue sea.

Chapter 5
"Where's Pittsburgh?"

Roberto spent the year 1954 in Montreal. It was not a happy time for him.

First of all, he could not speak English very well. The English he had learned from books in high school did not help him talk with his teammates.

Roberto was homesick for his family and for Puerto Rico. Not knowing much English made it all worse.

Also, he was black.

When Roberto came to Montreal, there were still laws in the southern part of the United States that kept black people and white people from doing things together.

Blacks could not eat in the same restaurants and could not stay in the same hotels as whites. Black children could not go to school with white children.

People with different-colored skin could not even use the same drinking fountains. White people could drink

Roberto had never seen separate drinking fountains until he came to the States. This kind of racial segregation is against the law now.

only from the fountains that said WHITE. Black people had to drink from the fountains marked COLORED.

When the Montreal Royals played in the South, Roberto and the other dark-skinned players could not room or eat with their white teammates. They had to stay in hotels and eat in restaurants in the black part of town.

In Puerto Rico, skin color did not matter as much as in the United States. There were more dark-skinned people in Puerto Rico than white people. And Roberto always had friends of different races.

Roberto could not get used to the way blacks were treated on the mainland.

"It's childish and unfair," Roberto said after his first road trip in the

South. He never stopped being angry at people who did not treat everyone the same.

But what made Roberto most unhappy was the treatment he was getting from the Montreal Royals.

Roberto was spending a lot of time on the bench. He wasn't getting his turn at bat. When he played well, he was pulled out of the game. When he played poorly, the manager left him in.

What was happening? Roberto couldn't figure it out.

At last one of the players who knew Spanish tried to explain.

"They are hiding you," he told Roberto. "They do not want other teams to see how well you play."

"*¿Por qué?* Why?" Roberto asked.

"Because," his teammate said,

"baseball rules say the Dodgers can't keep you in the minor leagues for more than one year. If they don't let you play in Brooklyn next year, another major league team can choose you to play for them. The Dodgers know there are many other teams that would like to have you — if they had a chance to see what a great hitter you are."

"Then, why don't the Dodgers let me play in Brooklyn if they think I'm so good?" Roberto asked.

His teammate looked embarrassed. "It may be because you are black," he said. "There are already four black men on the team. Maybe they are afraid that white people won't come to the games if there are more black players than white players on the field. I think that's why they want to keep you in Montreal for a while longer."

Roberto shook his head. He couldn't believe what he was hearing.

The Dodgers did try to keep Roberto hidden in Montreal, but the news got out anyway.

One day a scout from the Pittsburgh Pirates came to watch the Royals play. Roberto was in the lineup.

The scout saw Roberto smash a triple to left field and speed around the bases.

In the next inning, playing in right field, Roberto grabbed a ball off the fence and whipped it to third for a double play.

The manager took Roberto out of the game then, but it was too late. The Pirates knew about Roberto.

Every year baseball teams choose players who are not already signed up. This is called the *draft*. The team that has lost the most games the past season has the first choice.

In 1954 that team was the Pittsburgh Pirates, and they chose Roberto Clemente. The Dodgers had to let him go.

Roberto was in Puerto Rico when he heard the news. He was glad to be out of Montreal and playing for a major league team. But Pittsburgh?

"Where's Pittsburgh?" Roberto asked.

Roberto Clemente was soon to become famous for playing in the city of Pittsburgh for the Pirates.

But in 1954 Roberto had no idea where Pittsburgh was!

Chapter 6
"Puerto Rican Hot Dog"

Roberto was walking down a busy street in Pittsburgh. "Watch out, buddy," said a man carrying a ladder.

Roberto walked on. "Got the time, buddy?" another man asked him.

Roberto got on a bus and handed the driver a dollar bill. "Don't you have any change, buddy?" asked the bus driver.

Why was everyone calling him "buddy"? Were they making fun of him? Roberto angrily wondered. He still didn't know enough everyday English to understand that some people call you "buddy" when they don't know your name.

It was taking Roberto a long time to feel at home in Pittsburgh. For many reasons he was feeling bad. Roberto was having a hard time making friends with his teammates.

Also, the sun didn't shine nearly as much in Pittsburgh as it did in Puerto Rico, so Roberto often felt cold.

And the food was different. In Puerto Rico, people fried bananas and ate them like potatoes. In Pittsburgh, people cut them up and put them on cereal.

Also, even though there were no laws keeping blacks and whites apart in Pittsburgh, all the dark-skinned people seemed to live in one part of town anyway. And you hardly ever saw a black person and a white person together. And now Roberto was bothered by an injury.

It happened the winter before Roberto left for Pittsburgh. One of his brothers was very ill in the hospital in San Juan. Roberto was driving home from visiting his brother, when another car smashed into his at 60 miles per hour. The driver of the other car was drunk.

Roberto's back was hurt in the accident. He had trouble with his back the rest of his life. Sometimes he couldn't play baseball because it hurt too much.

His teammates did not always believe Roberto when he said he couldn't play. He looked like such a strong, healthy young man, it was hard to believe he had a bad back.

It took a long time for Roberto to win respect from his teammates and fame as a ballplayer.

In 1955, about the only person who seemed to believe in Roberto was Roberto himself. It wasn't until much later that the owner of the Pirates said he always knew Clemente would be an All-Star outfielder. He had such a great arm and "hit balls so hard you wouldn't believe it."

Roberto played his first major league game in a doubleheader against the Dodgers. He got the Pirates first hit and scored their first run that day.

Roberto was off to a good start, but he had many things to learn.

First, there was his batting. Roberto hardly ever got on base with a walk. He swung at almost any pitch.

"Hit only those pitches you like," the batting coach told him. But Roberto seemed to like just about every pitch that came across the plate.

He didn't always follow the signs the manager gave him. During one game, the manager told him to bunt. This would help the player on third base get home, tying the score. But instead, Roberto wanted to get a hit, and he struck out. Pittsburgh lost the game.

The manager fined Roberto twenty-five dollars. That was a lot of money back in 1955.

There was another time Roberto did not do what the manager wanted. The bases were loaded with the tying run on first when Roberto came up to bat. He swung. *Crack!* The ball flew deep

On June 6, 1956, Pirates' pitcher Ron Kline, is congratulated by teammates Roberto Clemente, Dale Long, and Frank Thomas as they celebrate their win over the Chicago Cubs.

into center field. The runners sped around the bases.

The manager wanted Roberto to stop at third base. There were no outs. Why take a chance trying to get to home plate?

But Roberto did not stop. He went right on. He whizzed by third base and slid safely into home just ahead of the ball.

It was an inside-the-park grand slam home run!

Did the manager fine him again? Of course not! Roberto had won the game for the Pirates. But some people said he was a show-off. A sports writer called him a "Puerto Rican hot dog."

Roberto did not understand. He thought the writer was making fun of his country. And he didn't like it.

"Puerto Rican hot dog?" he asked. "What does that mean? I am proud to be a Puerto Rican."

Chapter 7
"Beat 'Em Bucs"

With Roberto on the team, Pittsburgh was winning more games. He ended his second year as a Pirate with a .311 batting average. He got a good raise in pay and bought a beautiful new house for his parents.

People said he had the best arm in baseball. His throws were so fast, they looked like flying bullets. He could whip the ball from right field to first base so fast that he sometimes got two outs on one play — the batter, and the runner who had left first base.

In 1959, Pittsburgh was in second place in the National League.

In 1960, the team was in first place

for most of the season. The whole city was excited. Maybe this year they could win the National League championship and go on to play in the World Series. The last time the Pirates had played in the World Series was in 1927.

Fans filled the stadium for every game. They had a nickname for their team. They called them the "Bucs." That's short for buccaneers, another word for pirates.

Someone wrote a team song called "Beat 'Em Bucs." It became very popular. "Beat 'Em Bucs" signs hung everywhere.

The Pirates did win the National League title and went on to face the American League winners, the New York Yankees. It was one of the

Roberto Clemente gets ready to play the Yankees in the 1960 World Series.

most exciting World Series ever played.

The last of the seven games was played in Pittsburgh. The Series was tied, three games to three.

In the eighth inning, with the Pirates two runs behind, Roberto topped a ball and barely beat it out to first base. His hit helped put Pittsburgh back in the lead. The score was now 9–7. But the Yankees came back in the top of the ninth inning, tying the score.

Then in the bottom of the ninth, Pirate second baseman Bill Mazeroski hit a home run. That won the game and the World Series for the Pirates.

Pittsburgh exploded with joy. Fans all over the city rushed into the streets to celebrate.

Downtown Pittsburgh is at the

corner of a triangle formed by two rivers that flow together. The traffic on the bridges over the rivers was so jammed that people left their cars and walked across the bridges to join the party downtown.

The Pirate players had their own party at a hotel. But Roberto skipped it. He left the stadium and walked through the streets, talking to the people.

The happy crowds made him think of holidays in Puerto Rico. For the first time, Roberto Clemente felt really at home in Pittsburgh.

Chapter 8
"¡Arriba, Arriba!"

It was almost time for the game to begin. Why was Roberto Clemente gulping down spoonfuls of honey in the locker room?

In 1960, Roberto's batting average was an outstanding .314. He batted over .300 all season. Roberto was the only player on either team to get a hit in every game of the World Series.

Roberto said he would do even better in 1961. The Pirates' batting coach told him he could win the batting championship. Roberto said he would try.

One of the Pittsburgh players who

hit many home runs ate honey before each game to make himself stronger. So Roberto gave it a try.

The batting coach said he should use a heavier bat. Roberto began to swing a heavier and longer one. Also, he slowed up his swing and made sure to get plenty of wood on the ball.

Maybe it was the new batting style. Maybe it was the honey. Or both.

Halfway through the season Roberto was batting .357. It was the highest average in the league.

A new sound began to echo through the Pirate ball park.

"¡*Arriba. Arriba!*" the fans shouted when Roberto came up to bat.

Arriba means "Go!" in Spanish.

If Roberto made a great play in the field, the same cry would go up in the stadium: *"¡Arriba. Arriba!"* This sounded good to Roberto.

Then, Roberto was one of the few chosen to play for the National League in the All-Star game. He was picked as the starting right fielder.

In the All-Star game, he hit a triple in the second inning.

In the tenth inning of the game, the score was tied. Roberto smashed a single into right field to drive in the game-winning run.

He led the league in batting for the rest of the season and became the National League batting champion with a .351 average.

That winter in Puerto Rico, Roberto was eating at a fancy restaurant in San Juan. When he looked up from his dinner, he saw a row of noses pressed

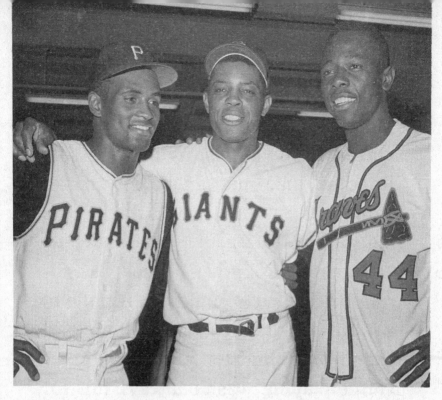

In 1961, Roberto Clemente, Hank Aaron, and Willie Mays were heroes of the National League's 5–4 victory over the American League.

flat against the glass window of the restaurant. Young baseball players of San Juan were trying to get a good look at their hero.

Wherever he went, kids crowded

around him. A black Puerto Rican had become a major league baseball star! Maybe they could do it, too.

During the 1960s, as time passed, Roberto became an even better ballplayer. By 1963, he was the Pirate's big star.

Roberto was known for being an all-round player. He could hit, run, field, and throw. And he made it all fun and exciting for the fans.

But playing wasn't always fun for Roberto. He had many aches and pains. In addition to his bad back, he had headaches, stomachaches, a bad leg, a bad elbow, and a hard time sleeping. How can Roberto be such a good player when he has so many things wrong with him? people asked.

Was it the super milk shake Roberto drank? It was made from ice cream, milk, eggs, bananas, pears or peaches, and orange juice, all tossed with ice in a blender. The milk shake cured many of his ills, Roberto said.

But still, Roberto was always seeing doctors and taking medicine.

On a winter day after the 1963 season, he was home in Puerto Rico. He made one of his many trips to the drugstore to get medicine. As Roberto went into the store, a tall, very pretty young woman came out.

"Who is she?" he asked the clerk.

"Vera Zabala," the clerk said. "Don't you know her? She's lived in this town all her life."

Roberto had never met her. But he wanted to see her again. He found out that Vera worked as a secretary downtown. He called her office and asked her out for lunch.

To his surprise, she said no. It was not the proper thing to do, she told Roberto.

Roberto had forgotten he was back in Puerto Rico. In Spanish-speaking countries, young men and women do not go out on dates by themselves.

So Roberto and Vera became friends the Puerto Rican way. Roberto asked a friend who knew Vera to invite her to a party. Roberto planned to go to this party just to meet her.

"Vera, this is Roberto Clemente," the friend said with a big grin.

About a year later Vera and Roberto were married in the big church that stood on the *plaza,* the town square, of their hometown.

Over a thousand people were invited to the wedding. Thousands more waited outside the church. They hoped to get a good look at the bride and groom.

Inside the church, Roberto stood at the altar, waiting for Vera to come down the aisle.

"Are you nervous?" the best man asked him.

"Who me, nervous?" said Roberto. "I feel great."

The best man laughed. "Then why don't you spit out your chewing gum?" he asked.

The happy couple, Roberto Clemente and Vera Christina Zabala, were married on November 14, 1964, in a town in Puerto Rico.

Maybe I am a bit nervous, Roberto thought as he got rid of his gum.

After the ceremony, when Vera and Roberto came out and waved to the crowd, shouts of *"¡Arriba!"* rang through the *plaza*.

Chapter 9
"Nowhere"

Roberto was a big hero in Puerto Rico. In 1964 and 1965, he won the National League batting title for the second and third times. Pittsburgh fans loved him.

But Roberto still did not get the Most Valuable Player (MVP) award. Sportswriters, who chose the most valuable player, said Roberto was not a power hitter. In 1965, he batted .329. But he only had 65 runs batted in (RBI's). Power hitters usually batted in about 100 runs.

Roberto made up his mind to become a power hitter. His goal was to hit 25 home runs and to bat in 115 runs. Again, he changed his batting style. He tried a new grip on the bat.

He started to hit more home runs. Soon pitchers walked him on purpose, just as they did with Henry Aaron or Willie Mays and the other power hitters.

At the end of the 1966 season, Roberto had 29 home runs and 119 RBI's. He also got his 2,000th hit, a home run that helped win a game. For the seventh year in a row, his batting average was above .300.

"If Roberto doesn't win the MVP this year," his manager said, "it will be a crime."

There was no crime. At last, Roberto was picked as the most valuable player in the National League.

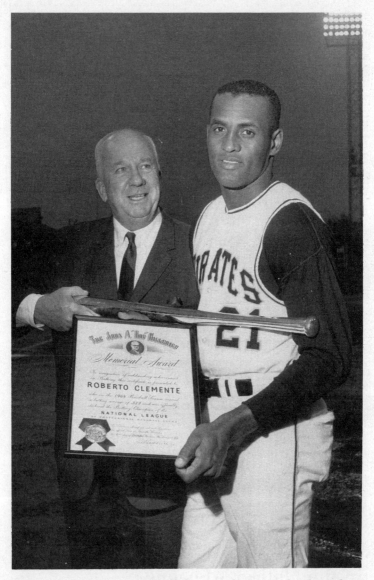

Roberto is presented with a plaque and silver bat for being the 1965 National League Batting Champion.

Why did it take so long for Roberto to win the award? He played in the major leagues for eleven years and won three batting championships before he was chosen.

Roberto always said that dark-skinned, Spanish-speaking ballplayers were not treated the same as players from the mainland.

Even with his popularity, reporters made fun of the way he spoke English. One sportswriter wrote that Roberto had said, "Me no like cold weather."

But Roberto did not talk like that. The newspapers often made his English sound worse than it really was.

Many people from Puerto Rico left the island and came north looking for a better life. There were not enough well-paying jobs to go around in Puerto Rico.

Because many Puerto Ricans were poor and did not have much schooling, Puerto Ricans were often treated badly on the mainland — even Roberto Clemente, baseball star.

One day Roberto and Vera were in a big furniture store in New York City. They wanted to buy nice furniture for their new house in Puerto Rico.

But the salesman tried to sell them the cheapest furniture in the store. Because the Clementes were black and Puerto Rican, the salesman thought they were too poor to buy good furniture.

Roberto and Vera found a couch they liked.

"Let me show you something

cheaper," the salesman said. "This one costs a lot."

Roberto had just been to the bank. He pulled five $1,000 bills out of his pocket. "Will it cost more than this?" he asked.

"Oh, no, no." The salesman became very polite and friendly. "May I ask your name, sir?"

"Roberto Clemente."

"*The* Roberto Clemente?"

Roberto nodded.

The salesman called everyone in the store to come around. A big fuss was made over the famous baseball player.

"Where shall we send the furniture, Mr. Clemente?" the salesman asked.

"Nowhere," Roberto said. "We'll buy our furniture someplace else."

And Roberto and Vera walked out of the store.

Roberto wanted all people to be treated the same.

He was very proud that he was the first Puerto Rican to win the MVP award. "Now," he said, "everyone will know Puerto Ricans are just as good as anyone."

Chapter 10
"¿Qué Hizo Roberto?"

In July 1970, a ninety-year-old Puerto Rican man and his wife stepped off a plane at the Pittsburgh airport. They had just had their first airplane ride.

The old man and woman were Melchor and Luisa Clemente. They were in town for a very special event. The Pirates were having a Roberto Clemente night at Pittsburgh's new stadium. The Clementes were there to attend the ceremony in which their son would be honored with gifts and speeches.

Roberto and Vera now had three young sons of their own — Roberto

Jr., Luis, and Enrique. The children sat with their mother and grandparents and watched the ceremony. Melchor and Luisa did not know enough English to understand all the speeches they heard that night. Like their grandparents, the boys did not understand everything that was said, either. But they all understood the love the crowd felt for Roberto. Great

Roberto holds his son, Enrique, just before the award ceremony.

cheers filled the stadium as Roberto stood in front of the microphone to speak.

Roberto began to talk, but his feelings of happiness got too much for him. He burst into tears.

"I haven't got the words to express my thanks," he said, "especially to my parents, who are old now."

Before Roberto's special day, his friends in Puerto Rico collected 300,000 signatures from people all over the island wishing him well. Then they tried to think of a good gift to send. But what could they buy for a man who already had everything?

"I know," said one of his friends. "We'll send Puerto Rican kids who are too poor to go to ball games to Pittsburgh for Roberto Clemente night. We'll let them see that someone like themselves can become important and famous." The chance to share his Puerto Rican pride with these children would be the best gift Roberto could ever receive.

Fifteen kids made the trip from Puerto Rico to Pittsburgh. They stayed at a fancy hotel with a swimming pool. At the ball game, they watched Roberto hit two solid singles and make some great catches.

When Roberto had finished playing in the middle of the ninth inning, the entire stadium began to ring with cheers for a black Puerto Rican who started playing baseball with a broomstick for a bat!

Roberto would get more and more cheers. In 1971, the Pirates won the

National League championship. They were to play the Baltimore Orioles in the World Series.

Everyone said the Orioles would win the series, most likely in four straight games. The Baltimore team had won the American League championship for four of the last six years.

The Pirates hadn't won the pennant since 1960, eleven years before.

The Orioles had four pitchers who had won more than twenty games each during the 1971 season. The Pirates did not have even one pitcher who had won as many as twenty games.

"The way everyone talks," Roberto said, "we should be playing in the Little Leagues."

The series began in Baltimore. The Orioles field was in terrible shape. It rained a lot that summer, and the Baltimore Colts football team had just played two games in the stadium.

The Orioles painted the bare spots on the turf green, so their field wouldn't look so bad on color TV.

Roberto took one look and said, "I'd rather play in a coal mine."

The Pirates lost the first two games. But Roberto got two hits in the first game and two more in the second.

Back in Pittsburgh on their own smooth turf, the Pirates did much better. They won the third game, with Roberto again getting two hits.

Game number four in Pittsburgh was the first World Series game ever played at night. About sixty million people watched on television. They saw Roberto come up to the plate and hit a powerful ball along the right field foul line.

Was it in or out? The umpire called it a foul ball. The fans in the Pittsburgh stadium didn't think so. Roberto didn't think so, either.

For five minutes the umpire and the Pirates yelled at each other on the field. The umpire did not change his mind. Roberto went back into the batter's box and belted a single into right field.

The Pirates won that game. The series was now tied, 2 – 2.

In the next game, Roberto drove in the winning run. The Pirates led the series, 3 – 2.

But now they had to leave their own field and go back to the soggy, torn-up turf in Baltimore for the rest of the games.

During the sixth game, Roberto went on with his hitting streak. He hit a triple in the first inning. Later, he hit his first World Series home run. Still, the Orioles beat the Pirates in the sixth game, tying the Series again.

It's a home run for Roberto!

The World Series was now down to the wire. Only one game was left to be played. It would decide the world championship.

Roberto hustled in every game as if he were a twenty-year-old rookie. But he was 37 years old in 1971. After a lot of thought, before the seventh and last game of the World Series, he told a Pittsburgh scout, "If we win this one, I'm going to quit baseball."

In the fourth inning, Roberto stepped into the batter's box and swung at the first pitch. He watched the ball sail over the 360-foot sign on the left field fence.

It was the game's first run. Later the Pirates scored again. Then Baltimore scored, but the Pirates held on. Pittsburgh won the game 2 – 1, and the World Series, four games to three!

In Puerto Rico, after every game, people asked each other, "*¿Qué hizo Roberto?*" That means "What did Roberto do?"

Here's what Roberto did in the 1971 World Series:

He batted .414.
He hit two home runs.
He fielded perfectly.
He ran like the wind.
He made two very hard "circus" catches.

People all over the country saw Roberto on television and read about him in the newspapers. "Now the whole world knows how I play,"

The Pittsburgh Pirates celebrate their victory as the new world champions.

Roberto said after the last game.

"Is it true you are going to quit baseball?" a reporter asked him.

Roberto shook his head. "I saw my wife as I ran off the field," he said. "She was crying. She said, 'Don't quit now. Baseball is your life.' And you know what," Roberto went on, "she's right. So I changed my mind. I'm not quitting baseball."

Chapter 11
"Go Get It!"

By 1972, only ten players in the history of baseball had gotten 3,000 hits.

Roberto badly wanted to be number 11. When the season began, he needed only 118 hits to reach the magic number. Roberto had gotten more than 118 hits every year he had played in the major leagues.

He won't have any trouble, said his family and friends. He'll make it.

With 3,000 hits, Roberto was sure to be the first Latin American ballplayer to be voted into baseball's Hall of Fame.

But during much of the season,

Roberto was either hurt or sick. He had the flu, a stomach virus, trouble with his heels. He lost ten pounds and had to wear a uniform that belonged to a thinner teammate.

By the middle of August, Roberto had missed almost half of the Pirates' games. People stopped talking about 3,000 hits. There just weren't enough games left in the season, they

Will he make 3,000 hits? Roberto holds a stack of mail from fans wishing him well.

thought. And nobody knew if he would be well enough to play again the next year.

With only 26 games left, Roberto still needed 25 hits to get to 3,000.

And then in September, he started to hit. Was there a chance he might get his 3,000th hit after all?

On September 28 in Philadelphia, Roberto faced Steve Carlton, the great Phillies pitcher. He hit a single to right field. It was hit number 2,999.

Right away, Roberto was taken out of the lineup. Everyone wanted him to get the 3,000th hit in Pittsburgh in front of the hometown fans.

The next night in Pittsburgh it was cold and rainy. Even so, 24,000 fans turned out to cheer Roberto on.

The Pirates were playing the New

York Mets. Tom Seaver was pitching. If Seaver could win this game, it would be another twenty-game season for the Mets' ace pitcher.

The crowd cheered loudly as Roberto walked up to the plate in the first inning.

One of Seaver's fastballs whizzed over the plate. Roberto swung hard but did not get much wood on the ball. It bounced over Seaver's glove. The second baseman ran in to grab it. The ball bounced off his glove. Roberto pulled up at first base.

Was the play a hit or an error? If the scorekeeper said it was an error, Roberto would not get his 3,000th hit.

It was so noisy in the stadium that only a few people heard the words,

"Error, second baseman," over the loudspeaker.

All eyes turned toward the scoreboard. For what seemed like a long time, there was nothing. Then the big H for hit went up.

The crowd cheered and clapped. The people were sure that Roberto had gotten hit number 3,000.

Suddenly, everyone became quiet. The H disappeared. An E for error went up on the scoreboard.

The scoreboard crew had not heard the call. They made a big mistake when they put up the H.

Boos sounded in the stadium. The Pirate fans felt cheated. So did Roberto. He was up three more times that night but could not get another hit.

"I'll be out there swinging again

tomorrow," Roberto said after the game.

The next day, Jon Matlock pitched for the Mets. That was bad news for Roberto. He had not hit one of Matlock's pitches all season.

In the first inning, Roberto struck out.

He came up to bat again in the fourth inning.

All-Star first baseman Willie Stargell was Roberto's best friend on the team.

He handed Roberto a bat.

"Go get it!" Stargell said.

And Roberto did! He sent a hard line drive bouncing off the left field wall for a double. The cheering that filled the stadium lasted for a full minute. On second base, Roberto tipped his helmet to the fans.

Willie Mays left the Mets dugout and came over to shake Roberto's hand.

On that day, September 30, 1972, there were just three men playing baseball who had 3,000 hits. They were Willie Mays, Hank Aaron, and now, Roberto Clemente.

Pittsburgh fans go wild as Roberto rests at second base (hands on hips) after his record-tying hit.

Chapter 12
"The Great One"

On December 23, 1972, the earth shook in Nicaragua.

Nicaragua is a small, poor country in Central America, not far from the island of Puerto Rico. Two days before Christmas in 1972, a terrible thing happened there.

A giant earthquake hit the biggest city in Nicaragua.

Over 6,000 people were killed. Another 20,000 were hurt. Thousands more were left homeless. People needed food, water, and medicines.

Roberto had been in Nicaragua a month before the earthquake.

While he was there, Roberto heard

about a fourteen-year-old boy who had a terrible thing happen to him. He had lost both his legs in an accident. The boy's parents had died. He needed artificial legs but had no money to pay for them.

A team in the Puerto Rican Winter League had raised part of the money the boy needed. Roberto himself gave the rest. He went to see the boy and told him he would be able to walk again. Roberto then returned to Pittsburgh.

When the earthquake hit Nicaragua, Roberto thought of his young friend. Had he lived through it? Was he all right? He had to find out.

Roberto also thought about the thousands of other people who had lost their homes and everything in them.

Caring about others who had less than he did was nothing new for Roberto. He had followed his father's teachings. He helped out other members of his family when they were in need. After his brother had died, he supported his nieces and nephews.

Roberto was kind to many people. One day during a game, the Pirates' announcer brought a deaf boy to meet Roberto. Roberto talked to the boy, using his hands and smiling.

Later, Roberto took one of his bats into the stands where the deaf boy was sitting. He gave him the bat.

On the side of the bat he wrote, "You don't have to be able to hear to play baseball and enjoy the game. Best wishes, Roberto Clemente."

So no one was surprised when

Roberto started helping people in Nicaragua after the earthquake.

He went from door to door in his neighborhood in San Juan asking for money. He spoke on radio and television asking the people of Puerto Rico to give money, food, clothes, and medicines.

He helped collect the supplies that came in. And he found ships and a plane to take the food and clothing to Nicaragua.

All during the Christmas holidays in 1972, Roberto helped pack the supplies into boxes.

Two planeloads of goods had already been flown to Nicaragua. Another would go on New Year's Eve, the last day of the year 1972.

New Year's Eve is an important

holiday in Puerto Rico. People come together from all over the island for family celebrations.

But Roberto decided to leave his family and fly to Nicaragua.

"I must see that the people who need the supplies really get them," he said.

And what had happened to his young friend who had lost his legs? This was his chance to find out.

The plane going to Nicaragua was a twenty-year-old propeller plane. Three weeks before, it had been in an accident. The brakes had not worked and the plane crashed into a wall. The propeller tips were badly bent.

Now, the brakes were fixed and the plane had new propellers. The plane was said to be ready to fly again.

It was supposed to take off at 4:00 P.M. in the afternoon.

But at 9:00 A.M. in the morning, the owner of the plane was still trying to find a crew to fly it to Nicaragua.

At last a pilot was found. There was a flight engineer, but he did not know much about that kind of plane.

They could not get a copilot. The owner of the plane no longer had a license to fly, but he decided to be the copilot anyway.

At 3:30 Vera took Roberto to the airport.

The plane was not ready.

Teenage helpers were loading the plane. It was already full, but they kept putting more and more boxes in. Everyone wanted to get the last of the supplies to Nicaragua.

"Is it safe?" Vera asked.

"Look, the plane is fine," the owner said. "It will be ready soon. If it were in bad shape I wouldn't go myself." And he climbed into the cockpit.

At 5:00 P.M. Roberto got onboard. Vera waved good-bye.

It wasn't until after 9:00 P.M. that the plane rolled down the runway toward the ocean for takeoff. The San Juan Airport is just a mile from the beach.

The plane was only in the air for a few seconds before there was a loud bang. Flames shot out from one of the engines.

The people in the control tower heard the pilot say, "I'm coming back around."

Then there were two more

explosions. The plane went off the radar screen in the control tower.

A man who lived in a house near the ocean heard a plane roaring overhead. He looked out the window and saw it flying so low, it almost hit the palm trees by the shore. Then he saw the plane fall into the ocean.

The man left the window to tell his son to call the police. When he came back, the plane had completely disappeared, sinking into the ocean.

It was after midnight when the phone rang at the Clementes' with the news about the plane crash. Vera rushed to the beach.

Bright orange flares lit up the night sky. Police cars parked on the beach and shone their headlights into the ocean. Coast Guard ships were in the water. Search crews looked for bodies and parts of the plane.

Nothing was found.

The next day the search went on. In the morning, the beach was full of people. Some were standing in the water. Some were holding small radios to their ears.

The search went on for weeks. Crowds were there every day. Every afternoon, Vera Clemente came and stood in the sand and watched.

Then one day she stopped coming.

The Coast Guard picked up parts of the plane. Later, Roberto's briefcase washed up on shore.

But Roberto's body was never found.

It was hard to believe Roberto was gone. "I expected him to swim to shore someplace," one of his Pirate teammates said.

High on the hills in Pittsburgh, there is a billboard that everyone can see from the Pirates' stadium. It is lit up brightly at night.

Most of the time it is a sign that sells beer.

After the plane crash, the sign said something else.

"Adiós amigo." Good-bye, friend.

Many wonderful things were said about Roberto. That he was the best ballplayer of his time. That he was the biggest hero Puerto Rico ever had.

Roberto became the first Latin American ballplayer voted into the Baseball Hall of Fame.

But there was something else about Roberto that was even more important. "He was a *good* man," said Willie Stargell.

On opening day of 1973, the Pirates scoreboard read, "Thank you, Roberto. We will never forget THE GREAT ONE."

The city of Pittsburgh and the Pittsburgh Pirates kept their promise. They did not forget Roberto.

In July 1994, more than twenty years after the plane crash in which he lost his life, a statue of Roberto Clemente was dedicated at the Pirates' stadium in Pittsburgh.

The statue was paid for by the people of Pittsburgh, and shows Roberto dropping his bat after hitting the ball. It must have been a good hit. He is just starting to run, as his eyes are fixed on the ball, far in the distance.

The statue tells us that Roberto lives on in our hearts and minds.

But he lives on in more than our memories. Roberto lives, too, in all the children that he helped.

Before he died, Roberto had plans

If you go to Three Rivers Stadium in Pittsburgh, you will see the statue of Roberto Clemente. Roberto's family (lower left) was there on the day the statue was dedicated, July 8, 1994.

Vera Clemente and her sons "break the ground" at a ceremony for the building of Roberto Clemente Sports City.

to build a "sports city" in Puerto Rico where the poor children of the island would have a chance to learn to play different kinds of sports.

After Roberto died, Sports City was built by his family. Over the years, thousands of children have gone there.

One baseball player who got his start at Sports City is Ruben Sierra, an outfielder for the Oakland Athletics. Sierra not only made it to the major leagues, but he also played in the 1994 All-Star game.

Sierra was a poor boy from a poor village in Puerto Rico. He says he would still be there today if it hadn't been for Roberto's Sports City.

When Sierra came up to bat during the All-Star game, millions of people were watching. They saw that he wore the number 21 on his uniform.

That was Roberto's number.

Sierra says, "He was the greatest. That's why I wear his number, in honor of him."

Baseball Basics

Here are some baseball terms used in this book. How many do you know?

All-Star Game   Every year, baseball fans vote for their favorite player at each position. These All-Stars make up two teams of players — one for the National League and one for the American League. About halfway through the baseball season, the two All-Star teams play each other in the All-Star Game.

American League and National League Major league teams are organized into two leagues, called the American and National Leagues. At the end of the baseball season, the winner of each league plays in the World Series for the world championship.

Baseball diamond   Three bases and home plate make up the corners of the baseball diamond, with second base opposite home plate.

Baseball Hall of Fame   Sportwriters from all over the United States choose the very greatest players to be in the Hall of Fame. The Hall of Fame itself, in Cooperstown, New York, is a museum and library all about baseball. People say the game of baseball was invented at Cooperstown.

There is a plaque in the museum for each player who is a member. Players cannot be chosen until five years after they stop playing. (Roberto Clemente was an exception to this rule. He was inducted into the Hall of Fame in August 1973, eight months after his death.)

Batting average   This is the number of hits a player gets compared to the number of times he's at bat. If a player has three hits for every ten times he's at the plate, he is hitting .300. Any average higher than .300 is good. Roberto's lifetime batting average was .317.

Bunt   A bunt is a very short hit. The batter does not swing at the ball. Instead, he just reaches out and taps the ball with his bat.

Double   A hit that allows the batter to go to second base is a double.

Double play   A double play takes place when two players are put out as a result of one batter's at bat. Roberto took part in many double plays because he threw the ball so fast.

Error   Error means mistake. If a batter gets on base because a fielding player drops the ball or makes some other mistake, the play is counted as an error. It does not count as a hit for the batter.

Lineup   The nine players that bat in the game are said to be "in the lineup." The other players on the team sit in the dugout and are said to be "on the bench."

Major and minor leagues   The major leagues are the big leagues in which the best players compete. Many minor league teams are owned by major league clubs. These teams are sometimes called "farm teams" because they get young players ready for big league competition.

The Montreal Royals, for which Clemente played in 1954, was a farm team for the Brooklyn Dodgers. The Dodgers, of course, are now in Los Angeles, and Montreal now has its own major league team, the Expos.

MVP   These letters stand for most valuable player. Each year, certain sportwriters choose one player they think is the best in the National League and one in the American League. Roberto won the National League MVP award in 1966.

Pennant   The team from each major league that wins the most games wins the championship. In the early days of baseball the winning team used to get a small flag, called a pennant. "Winning the pennant" is another way of saying "winning the championship."

RBIs   These initials stand for runs batted in. Every time a batter gets a hit and a runner on base gets to home plate, that run counts as a "run batted in" for the batter. Power hitters, who hit lots of doubles, triples, and home runs, will have many RBIs on their records. Roberto wanted to have lots of RBIs and worked hard to make himself a power hitter.

Signs   During a game, the team's manager often tells the players what to do by using secret hand movements instead of speech. If a manager wants a player to bunt, he will make certain movements with his fingers. These signs tell the batter to bunt the ball.

Single   A hit that allows the batter to get on first base is a single.

Starting player   A player who is in the lineup when the game begins is called a starting player.

Strikeout   There are three ways to get a strike: (1) the first two times a batter hits the ball out of bounds (foul) are called strikes; (2) when a batter does not swing at a ball that is pitched over home plate in his "strike zone"; and (3) when the batter swings at a pitch and misses. No matter how the strike is made, as we know, three strikes and you're out!

Strike zone   This is the area in which a pitcher must place the ball: over home plate, below the batter's shoulders, and above his knees.

Top a ball   A player tops a ball when he hits it with the bottom side of his bat. A ball that is topped hits the ground near home plate and does not go very far.

Triple   A hit that allows the batter to go all the way to third base is a triple.

Walk   One way of getting to first base without getting a hit. A batter walks (is awarded first base) when the pitcher throws four "balls" — pitches that do not go over home plate or are either higher than the batter's shoulders or lower than his knees.

Whiff   This is what a batter does when he swings at the ball and misses. Say "whiff" out loud. Doesn't it sound like the noise a bat makes when you swing and miss?

World Series Every year, at the end of the baseball season, the winners of the two major leagues (the National League and the American League) play each other. The first team that wins four games wins the World Series.

Know Your Spanish

These Spanish words and phrases are used in this book:

Adiós amigo — Good-bye, friend
Arriba — Go
Hasta mañana — See you tomorrow
Plaza — Open space in the middle of a town
¿Por qué? — Why?
¿Qué hizo Roberto? — What did Roberto do?
Uno más — One more

ROBERTO WALKER CLEMENTE

Born August 18, 1934, in Carolina, Puerto Rico.
5'11", 175 lbs. Bats right, throws right.
Elected Hall of Fame 1973.

Regular Season

Year	GP	BA	AB	H	2B	3B	HR	R	RBI	SB	PO	A	E	DP
1955	124	.255	474	121	23	11	5	48	47	2	253	18	6	5
1956	147	.311	543	169	30	7	7	66	60	6	274	17	13	2
1957	111	.253	451	114	17	7	4	42	30	0	272	9	6	1
1958	140	.289	519	150	24	10	6	69	50	8	312	22	6	3
1959	105	.296	432	128	17	7	4	60	50	2	229	10	13	1
1960	144	.314	570	179	22	6	16	89	94	4	246	19	8	2
1961	146	.351	572	201	30	10	23	100	89	4	256	27	9	5
1962	144	.312	538	168	28	9	10	95	74	6	269	19	8	1
1963	152	.320	600	192	23	8	17	77	76	12	239	11	11	2
1964	155	.339	622	211	40	7	12	95	87	5	289	13	10	2
1965	152	.329	589	194	21	14	10	91	65	8	288	16	10	1
1966	154	.317	638	202	31	11	29	105	119	7	318	17	12	3
1967	147	.357	585	209	26	10	23	103	110	9	273	17	9	4
1968	132	.291	502	146	18	12	18	74	57	2	297	9	5	1
1969	138	.345	507	175	20	12	19	87	91	4	226	14	5	1
1970	108	.352	412	145	22	10	14	65	60	3	189	12	7	2
1971	132	.341	522	178	29	8	13	82	86	1	267	11	2	4
<u>1972</u>	<u>102</u>	<u>.312</u>	<u>378</u>	<u>118</u>	<u>19</u>	<u>7</u>	<u>10</u>	<u>68</u>	<u>60</u>	<u>0</u>	<u>199</u>	<u>5</u>	<u>0</u>	<u>2</u>
18yrs	2433	.317	9454	3000	440	166	240	1416	1305	83	4696	266	140	42

League Championship Series

Year	GP	BA	AB	H	2B	3B	HR	R	RBI	SB	PO	A	E	DP
1970	3	.214	14	3	0	0	0	1	1	0	7	0	0	0
1971	4	.333	18	6	0	0	0	2	4	0	12	0	0	0
<u>1972</u>	<u>5</u>	<u>.235</u>	<u>17</u>	<u>4</u>	<u>1</u>	<u>0</u>	<u>1</u>	<u>1</u>	<u>2</u>	<u>0</u>	<u>10</u>	<u>0</u>	<u>0</u>	<u>0</u>
3yrs	12	.265	49	13	1	0	1	4	7	0	29	0	0	0

World Series

Year	GP	BA	AB	H	2B	3B	HR	R	RBI	SB	PO	A	E	DP
1960	7	.310	29	9	0	0	0	1	3	0	19	0	0	0
<u>1971</u>	<u>7</u>	<u>.414</u>	<u>29</u>	<u>12</u>	<u>2</u>	<u>1</u>	<u>2</u>	<u>3</u>	<u>4</u>	<u>0</u>	<u>15</u>	<u>0</u>	<u>0</u>	<u>0</u>
2yrs	14	.362	58	21	2	1	2	4	7	0	34	0	0	0

ROBERTO WALKER CLEMENTE
PITTSBURGH N. L. 1955-1972

MEMBER OF EXCLUSIVE 3,000-HIT CLUB. LED
NATIONAL LEAGUE IN BATTING FOUR TIMES.
HAD FOUR SEASONS WITH 200 OR MORE HITS
WHILE POSTING LIFETIME .317 AVERAGE AND
240 HOME RUNS. WON MOST VALUABLE PLAYER
AWARD 1966. RIFLE-ARMED DEFENSIVE STAR
SET N. L. MARK BY PACING OUTFIELDERS IN
ASSISTS FIVE YEARS. BATTED .362 IN TWO
WORLD SERIES, HITTING IN ALL 14 GAMES.

Roberto was the first Latin American player to be voted into baseball's Hall Of Fame. This plaque lists the highlights of his 17-year career.